For Hilde and
Wim's grandchildren, Eline,
Lente, Wolf and Orin
~A.M.

For Jon
~C.W.

First American edition published 2001 by
Crocodile Books
An imprint of Interlink Publishing Group, Inc.
99 Seventh Avenue, Brooklyn, NY 11215 and
46 Crosby Street, Northampton, Massachusetts 01060
Text © 2001 Anne Mangan
Illustrations © 2001 Catherine Walters
Published simultaneously in Great Britain by Little Tiger Press
All rights reserved
Printed in and bound in Belgium
ISBN 1-56656-376-3

To request our complete full-color catalog,
please call us toll free at **1-800-238-LINK,** visit our website at
www.interlinkbooks.com, or write to: **Interlink Publishing**
46 Crosby Street, Northampton, MA 01060
e-mail: info@interlinkbooks.com

The Monkey
who
Wanted the
MOON

by
Anne Mangan

illustrated by
Catherine Walters

Crocodile Books, USA

An imprint of Interlink Publishing Group, Inc.
New York • Northampton

Simia lived in the jungle with her family and all the other animals. They had a great time playing among the trees.

At first Simia's mother would hold her by her tail so that she would not stray too far. The little monkey did not like this at all. She wanted to go into the jungle and poke her small nose into everything.

Simia grew quickly, and soon she was big
enough to wander about on her own.
She loved all the beautiful things she saw.
She loved them so much that she wanted
them for herself.

One day she was out exploring when
she saw something shining and yellow.
She put out her hand and grabbed it . . .

Aaagh!

It was a cactus
flower, and the
sharp thorns on it
hurt. Simia ran back
to her mother crying.
"Don't grab at everything
you see," her mother said,
rubbing Simia's poor, sore hand.

It wasn't long before Simia had forgotten all about the
cactus. She was off again, looking for something new.
In the tall grass, she saw what seemed even more
beautiful than the cactus. She reached out her
hand to take it . . .

Grrrrr!

A jaguar with golden eyes and a very bad temper jumped out, snarling fiercely.

Simia ran and ran and didn't stop until she noticed something on the ground with a zig-zag pattern. She touched it, and it was warm and dry.
"What a lovely toy!" she thought. She tried to pick it up, and it moved . . .

Sssss!

It was a snake! It uncoiled itself and shot into the air, its tongue flicking from side to side.

Simia ran and ran until she came to a shady tree. There, above her, she saw a coconut even bigger than herself. "Oh, I must have that," she cried. She climbed up the tree, reached out for the coconut, and gave it a push . . .

Zzzzz!

Wzzzzzz!

A crowd of angry wasps
swarmed around Simia,
because the coconut wasn't
a coconut at all. It was a
wasps' nest! Simia ran back
to her mother. She had been
stung all over.
"Silly," said her mother, gently rubbing
Simia's left ear, the only place that didn't hurt.

Simia was soon climbing
another tree, the wasps
forgotten. There, among the
branches, she found a nest with
some amazing white things in it.
She didn't think they belonged
to anyone, so she stretched
out her hand to scoop
them up. Then, just
as she reached
the nest . . .

Squaaawwk!

"You leave my eggs alone!"
shouted a bird. "You little
monster, you!"
"I'm a little monkey, not a little
monster," chattered Simia, before
clambering down the tree again, away
from the bird's sharp beak.

Simia thought she would keep away
from birds, but she still loved
climbing trees. She sniffed and
snuffled along until she came to
a beautiful tree with pale green
leaves. Up, up she went, until
suddenly she saw something
bright red amidst the pale green.
How she wanted that lovely red
thing! Simia took it in her fingers
and gave it a pull . . .

Screeech!

The red thing was a parrot's tail!
"How would you like me to pull *your* tail?"
asked the parrot angrily.
"I wouldn't," cried Simia, and away she
scampered while her tail was still safe!

Down by the lake, Simia saw something else . . .

It was a gentle blue flower
without a single thorn. Simia
picked it and sat in the sun,
holding it carefully. It was her
very own flower.

She carried it back home, but by
the time she reached there, the flower
had wilted. It flopped over her hand,
no longer beautiful.

"If you had left it where you found it, it would
be beautiful still," said her mother.

Feeling cross and sad, Simia
went back to the lake,
where she saw . . .

the other little monkeys playing with a lovely stone.
Simia wanted it so badly, that she ran towards
them and grabbed it.
She ran and ran, with the other monkeys
chasing her, chattering angrily.

Before they could catch her, Simia threw the stone
into the lake.

Now no one could have the stone.
Angry and sad, Simia crept back home again.

That evening, Simia's mother took her out in the
moonlight. They climbed the tallest tree and
Simia looked up to where the sky was filled with
stars. There was the moon, too, big and round.

Simia wanted the moon. She left her mother
and reached out to grab it . . .

but she tipped over and
fell down and down until
a big bird caught her and
took her back to her mother.
"I wanted that lovely, shiny,
round thing," sobbed Simia.
"You can't grab the moon," said
her mother. "Some things are for
yourself, some things are for others,
and some things, like the moon, are
for everyone to share. You don't have
to own things to enjoy them."

Simia looked up at the big,
bright moon and found
that she could enjoy it
just by looking at it.
Suddenly she was
the happiest little
monkey in the
world.